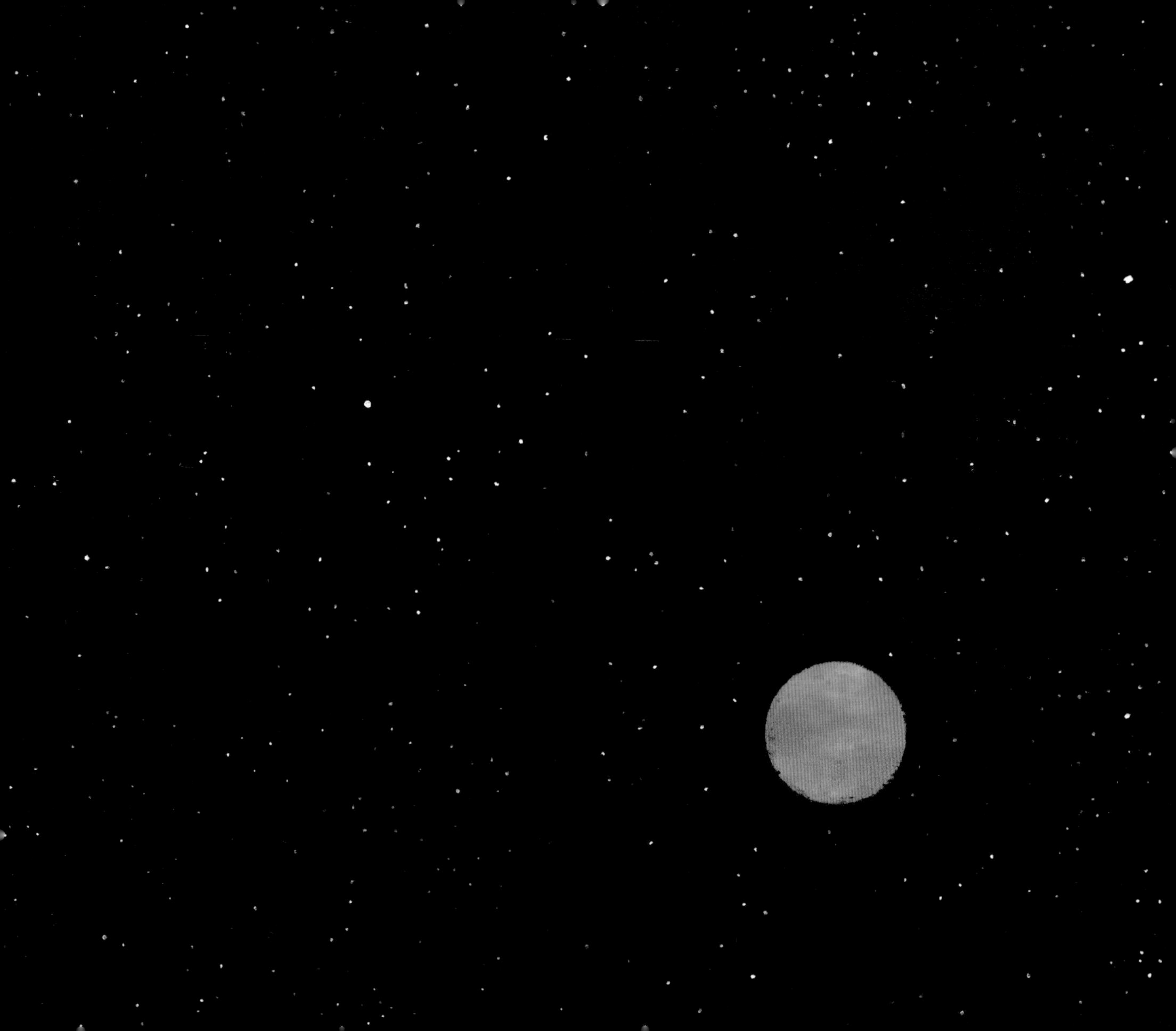

To the curiosity inside all of us—SS
For my parents, Marjory and Tom Ross—AJR

W

PENGUIN WORKSHOP
An Imprint of Penguin Random House LLC, New York

Copyright © 2019 by Penguin Random House LLC. All rights reserved. Published by Penguin Workshop, an imprint of Penguin Random House LLC, New York. PENGUIN and PENGUIN WORKSHOP are trademarks of Penguin Books Ltd, and the W colophon is a registered trademark of Penguin Random House LLC. Manufactured in China.

Visit us online at www.penguinrandomhouse.com.

Library of Congress Cataloging-in-Publication Data is available upon request.

ISBN 9781524791223   10 9 8 7 6 5 4 3 2 1

BIRTHDAY ON MARS!

by Sara Schonfeld • illustrated by Andrew J. Ross

Penguin Workshop

My name is Curiosity, and I live on Mars.

Good morning, Mars!

My friends from Earth sent me here
to explore the entire planet.

No humans have ever been here before. Isn't that cool?

You might think it's lonely here.
But I talk to my friends on Earth every day.

I tell them what I've learned and send them pictures of what I've seen.

Today there's one big thing to share with my friends on Earth
I should send the message now.
Hey, Earth!

It's My Birthday!

Now I have to get ready to celebrate my birthday.
I should take a picture to share with my friends.

Oops—I made a dust cloud!
I guess I should slow down.
I'm just so excited!

I'm sending them the photo now. It takes a while because I am very far away. While I wait, I'll sing myself a song.

Happy birthday to me,
happy birthday to me.
Happy birthday, Curiosity.
Happy birthday to me.

I know we can't be on the same planet for my birthday,
but we can still celebrate together.
And my birthday is the perfect time to celebrate curiosity!

We should all be curious—about everything!

Curious about new places we've never been.
Curious about new things we haven't learned yet.

So even if I'm lonely, I know
I'm never really alone.

Because I have billions of
friends back on Earth.
And they're celebrating
curiosity every day.

Especially today. Because today
is extra-special.

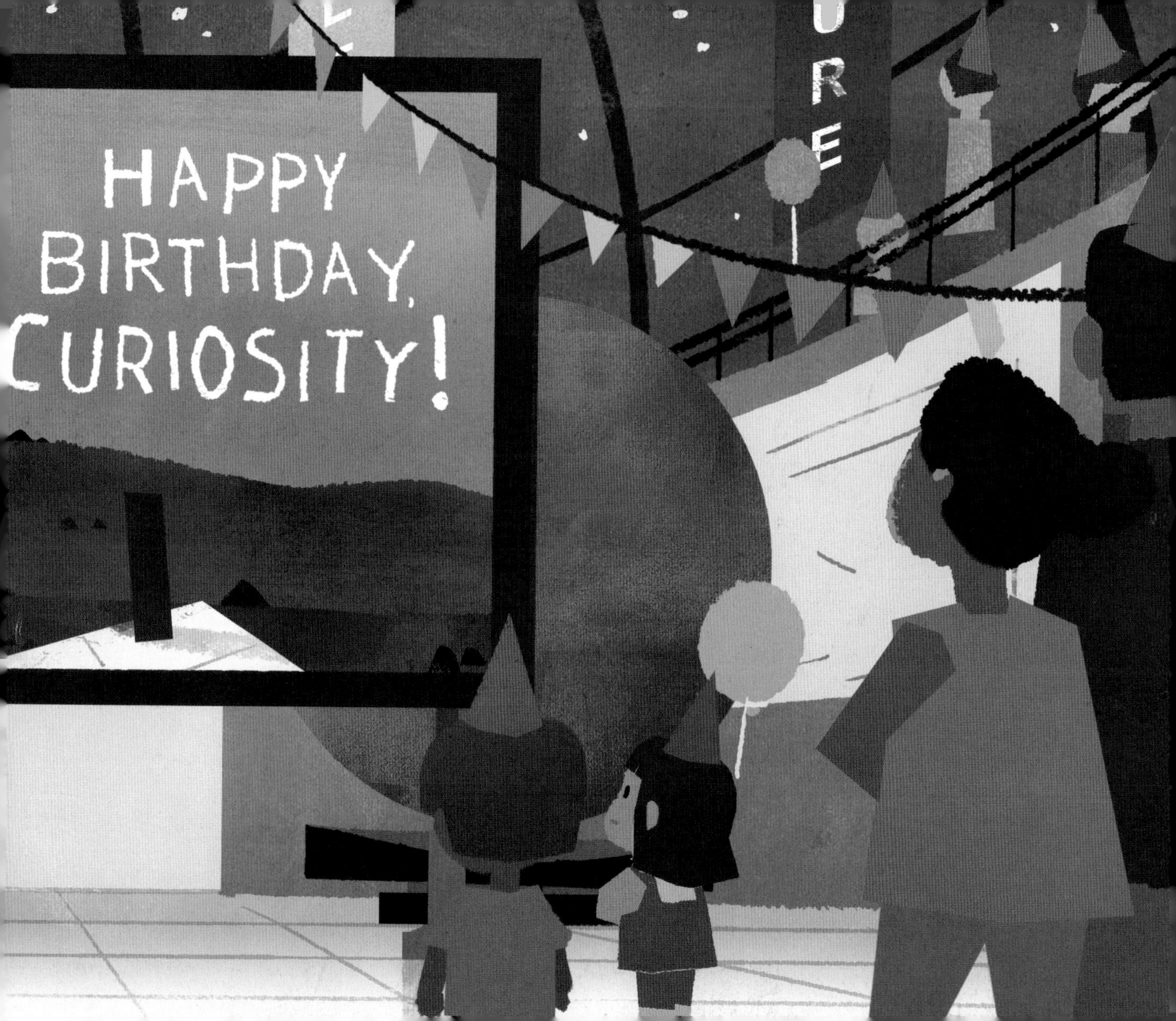
HAPPY BIRTHDAY, CURIOSITY!

CURIOUS ABOUT MARS?

- Mars is one of our closest neighbors. But it's not that close. On average, it is **140 million miles** away from Earth. To travel that distance on Earth, you would have to go **all the way around the world—more than 5,000 times**!

- Earth is much larger than Mars. In fact, Mars is **half** the size of Earth.

- The National Aeronautics and Space Administration (NASA) has been sending robots called rovers to Mars since 1997. Technically Curiosity isn't alone, because **Sojourner**, **Spirit**, and **Opportunity** are still on Mars, too.

- The Curiosity rover really did sing itself **"Happy Birthday"** after its first year on Mars, back on August 5, 2013.

- Curiosity welcomed a new sibling named **InSight** on November 26, 2018. InSight will dig deep beneath the surface of the planet, so we can continue to learn even more about Mars.